To Conov
All the
from Bruno
X

SHAKESPEARE: THE ETERNAL POET
PART ONE

BRUNO PATRON

PATRON
OF THE ARTS

Newry, Co. Down, Northern Ireland
www.patronofthearts.co.uk
brunopatron@hotmail.com

ACKNOWLEDGEMENTS

I would like to thank my mother Maura Erskine, my uncle, Thomas Erskine, and friends, Mary Anne Thompson, Joanne Kiley, Julia Dunlop and Mairead Mulkern for all of their invaluable support.
I would also like to extend a special *thank you* to the actor Vincent Regan for his words of encouragement to me many years ago that inspired me to complete this publication.

First published in Northern Ireland by Patron of the Arts 2010

ISBN 978-0-9564982-0-5

©2010 Bruno Patron
All rights reserved. No part of this publication may be reproduced, stored in a material system, or transmitted in any form, or by any means electronic, mechanical, photocopying, recording or otherwise, without prior written permission from Bruno Patron.

CONTENTS

Introduction

Imagine today you write a beautiful poem about a particular aspect of human nature that has inspired you. It could be about the love you feel for someone, the adversity or trauma you once experienced, and how you overcame such personal struggles. The poem could be about absolutely anything that affects you in someway whilst you live your life, and having carefully chosen a selection of words from the thousands of words you could choose from, you read the poem back to yourself and feel satisfied that you have written something people will relate to. Family and friends read your poem and are amazed by how you have captured that particular aspect of human nature perfectly. A few more people read it and concur to the uncanny insight your poetic verse possesses. Someone posts your poem onto the Internet and millions of people around the world read your poem, easily identifying with your verse because they feel, or have felt the feelings you have written about so eloquently.

It is not just a *good* poem, it is a *magnificent* poem, and because of its magnificence transcends your mortal time, and skips effortlessly through the generations and the centuries that follow; read by millions of people in the future – your words speaking to them individually in a deeply personal way.

No doubt those future generations of people will read your poem with wonder because you lived hundreds of years previously when the world was socially and technologically different - a period of Time forever locked away into *historical era*. Your poem has become a 'timeless classic,' proving to people of the future that you were no different to them in *your* time as they will see *you* as the same in *theirs*.

Being human is about being trapped in the feelings of 'being human' in an imperfect world where we will always possess the myriad of feelings that make us unique in the animal kingdom, but not so different amongst our own kind regardless of whichever generation is the incumbent at the time.

It could happen if you were ever to apply yourself
to writing that magnificent poem.

Shakespeare did exactly that over four hundred years ago, but he did not post just one poem to history, he posted one hundred and fifty four when they were first published in 1609, and these have been published over and over again as the centuries passed onwards to our present day. They can also be read on the many active websites that abound the Internet; his poems more easily available to anyone than at anytime before.

So, why would anyone want to read Shakespeare's *Sonnets*?

Shakespeare's work is not everyone's ideal for brain 'switch off' entertainment, his language has become too remote and complicated for many modern ears and eyes to understand. He has been practically monopolised by the intelligent and the cultural echelons of society who appear to understand him better, and this over the centuries has moved the greater population further away from the real Shakespeare – an ordinary man of the people who wrote plays and poems for ordinary people. It has been nearly forgotten that he was a great poet; the popularity of Shakespeare's plays has overshadowed this aspect of his creative mastery.

The Sonnets are different to Shakespeare's plays in several ways.

Firstly the language he uses is that of a man speaking to any man or woman. The obligatory 'thee,' 'thy,' 'thou' and 'hath' are there, but his language is not that dissimilar to our own today, and can be understood a lot easier than many of his plays.

Secondly his plays are meant for a wider audience in a theatre environment, entertainment for a mass audience so to speak. In the *Sonnets* Shakespeare is 'talking' about the feelings he felt and knows you will feel also, and when he compiled the work for its first publication he was clearly meaning to engage in a *one to one* between *himself* and *you* personally.

Thirdly, the *Sonnets* follow a constant rhythm throughout, known as the 'iambic pentametre,' so each poem jolts along like a pop song with a drum beat in the background, unlike his plays where the dialogue is interspersed with a dazzling assortment of many different rhythms.

Finally Shakespeare has used the poetic genre to show us the many faces of the human being without being over complicated by plot, or the required drama of a full blown theatrical show. These sonnets are one man bearing his inner self, emotional warts and all, for *you*, the reader to contemplate upon, and having read his poems see that you too have the same human qualities of strength and weakness he once possessed. The poems are not meant to extol the virtues of religious faith, God and Jesus Christ (neither of whom get a mention in any of the poems*), they are a journey into love, hate, jealousy, anger, sexual desire, contradiction, mortality, and many more elements that make us human beings.

I first read a Shakespeare sonnet when I was at school in the 1970's. As an adolescent I was too inexperienced in life to understand what was being expressed, but the language of his poems bounced along with a colour and stride that brought images into my youthful mind that seemed to breathe life and pictures into words written several centuries ago, and the fact that poetry

---

*In Sonnet Fifty Eight Shakespeare starts the poem with "That god forbid," but he uses this as a cliché comment in the same way that "oh my god" is commonly used today as a means to express surprise or shock, and not meant as a statement of religious commitment.

of a different era long passed still worked as valid pieces of Art was exciting and inspiring to me, someone born into the world over three hundred and sixty years after Shakespeare wrote them, vindication that his *Sonnets* are "not of an age, but for all time," Eternal Poetry by an Eternal Poet.

Shakespeare's *Sonnets* reveal the power of human nature in love and our interaction with other men and women, as well as the frailty of the human condition to growing older and our own mortality. Their poetic insight to the complexities of who we are means they can still have a place in people's lives today- if they take a little 'time out' to read them.

A great deal has been said and written about the *Sonnets* over the centuries by Shakespearian experts and critics alike, and many of their words have become a historical marker for us to glimpse into their society's level of broadmindedness and acceptance to the underlying implied themes covered in the poems. But I do not think that the *Sonnets* importance and relevance is as a consequence of what has been written about them, or even how they have been judged through history; their importance and relevance has continued through the centuries because generations of History's people read them, and personalised the work to themselves individually, in the same way we may relate to the lyrics of a pop song personally because the lyrical sentiment reminds us of what we have experienced ourselves. Shakespeare's *Sonnets* are a personal insight into the many aspects of the human condition that applies to us all, and the only truly qualified person to judge them is *you*, and if there is one thing that can be said about the *Sonnets* they are poems *you* will take personally.

They are poetic verses that have courted controversy, heated debate, and admiration, but they remain hundreds of years after their first publication as ambiguous as ever, where they beg many more questions than answers, but they will always surprise us and not just because they are written by one of Literature's greatest minds, but because the work's themes causes us to confront our own personal prejudices, beliefs, feelings and fears, and this aspect of the *Sonnets* I will investigate in *Shakespeare, The Eternal Poet. Part Two.*

What is a sonnet?

The word *Sonnet* comes from the Italian *'sonetto'* and Occitan *'sonet'* meaning *"little song,"* and was a lyrical poetic format used by poet's centuries before Shakespeare.

A sonnet is a fourteen line poem with a consistent rhyming sequence, structure and rhythm. Each four line section is called a *quatrain*, two quatrains are called an *octet* and the remaining six lines are known as the *sestet*.

The sonnet form became greatly refined by the Italian Poet Francesco Petrarch (1304-1374) by taking a constant rhythmic sequence of the last word in each line as *abba abba cdcdcd or cdecde*. This type of poetic rhythm has become known as the *Petrarchan*.

The English poet Thomas Wyatt (1503-1543) introduced this poetic form into England in the early sixteenth century and became very popular with poets and the public alike. William Shakespeare's sonnets differ from the Petrarchan form by changing the octet and the sestet rhyming sequence to *abab cdcd efef gg*. The final two lines are called the *Rhyming Couplet*. It is within the Rhyming Couplet Shakespeare would sum up the argument of the sonnet, or introduce a new and sometimes contradictory idea.

Sonnet Eighteen

Shall I compare thee to a summer's day?
Thou art more lovely and more temperate:
Rough winds do shake the darling buds of May,
And summer's lease hath all too short a date:
Sometime too hot the eye of heaven shines,
And often is his gold complexion dimmed,
And every fair from fair sometime declines,
By chance, or nature's changing course untrimm'd:
But thy eternal summer shall not fade,
Nor lose possession of that fair thou ow'st,
Nor shall death brag thou wandr'st in his shade,
When in eternal lines to time thou grow'st,
    So long as men can breathe or eyes can see,
    So long lives this, and this gives life to thee.

Shall I compare you to a summer's day? You are more lovely and sweet natured. Spring winds shake May's blossoms and summertime is all but too short. Summer can be too hot and sunny, but that sunshine can also be obscured by clouds, and every beautiful thing *('fair from fair')* at some point has to grow older *('declines')* either by accident or nature's naturally changing course. However your eternal beauty shall not fade, nor ever lose possession of the beauty you owe to nature, nor shall your beauty walk in the shadow of death as time moves eternally forward and you grow older. So long as men can breathe and have eyes to see, so long as my sonnets exist (and can be read) these will always give life to you.

Sonnet Twenty Four

Mine eye hath play'd the painter and hath steel'd,
Thy beauty's form in table of my heart,
My body is the frame wherein 'tis held,
And perspective it is best Painter's art.
For through the Painter must you see his skill,
To find where your true Image pictured lies,
Which in my bosom's shop is hanging still,
That hath his windows glazed with thine eyes:
Now see what good turns eyes for eyes have done,
Mine eyes have drawn thy shape, and thine for me
Are windows to my breast, where-through the Sun
Delights to peep, to gaze therein on thee;
    Yet eyes this cunning want to grace their art,
    They draw but what they see, know not the heart.

My eyes have become the painter and with my steel tipped pen, writer's table and heart felt emotions have described your beautiful form; and this is contained within the frame of my body, and it is through correct perspective of art (inspiration) that keeps my feelings in proportion. It is through the artist's skill can you see the true nature of your own image, and in the gallery of my breast this picture hangs, and the windows shine more brightly because your image hangs there. Yours and mine eyes have drawn each other's shape truthfully (we know each other so well), and this pleases me greatly like the sun peeping through the window to look upon you. There are artists who want to paint you so that your beauty can show off their artistic skill, but they can only draw on what they see (theirs is a shallow artistic expression), but they will never know the full extent of the heartfelt truth.

Sonnet Sixty Four

When I have seen by Time's fell hand defaced
The rich proud cost of outworn buried age,
When sometime lofty towers I see down-raz'd,
And brass eternal slave to mortal rage.
When I have seen the hungry ocean gain
Advantage on the kingdom of the shore,
And the firm soil win of the watery main,
Increasing store with loss, and loss with store.
When I have seen such interchange of state,
Or state itself confounded, to decay,
Ruin hath taught me thus to ruminate
That Time will come and take my love away.
  This thought is as a death which cannot choose
  But weep to have, that which it fears to lose.

When I have seen time deface the rich societies of a now buried age. When I have seen great monuments razed to the ground becoming metal of no value because of the rage of mortals. When I have seen the ocean cast up its tsunami destroying the land of its firm soil gaining in size with the land mass's loss, and then receding to its original size, the land gaining once more what it had lost. When I witnessed such natural changes, or even when the land has become decayed, such ruins therefore made me meditate, that one day Time will come to take you away from me (or my love for you will be taken away when I die). This thought is deathly, and not from choice, all there will be are tears because of the fear of such a loss.

Sonnet Ninety One

Some glory in their birth, some in their skill,
Some in their wealth, some in their body's force,
Some in their garments though new-fangled ill:
Some in their hawks and hounds, some in their horse.
And every humour hath his adjunct pleasure,
Wherein it finds a joy above the rest,
But these particulars are not my measure,
All these I better in one general best.
Thy love is better than high birth to me,
Richer than wealth, prouder than garments' cost,
Of more delight than hawks and horses be:
And having thee, of all men's pride I boast.
    Wretched in this alone, that thou mayst take,
    All this away, and me most wretched make.

Some glorify in their birth, some are glorified in their skill, some in their wealth, even some by their body's power, some in their fashion, even if poorly made, some in the finest birds and hounds they keep, and some in the horses they rear. Every character trait (*'humour'*) can be happily joined together (*'adjunct'*) where a certain type of joy is felt on a higher plain to anything else experienced. These are not the particular aspects of human nature I subscribe to, I better all these pleasures in one over all view, your love is better than any high birth, richer than any wealth, better fashion than any expensive garment, more delightful than any fine birds of prey or horses. By having you in my life I will proudly boast to every man with pride, and how wretched it would be if you were to take all this away, and how wretched that would make me feel.

Sonnet One Hundred and Six

When in the chronicles of wasted time,
I see descriptions of the fairest wights,
And beauty making beautiful old rhyme,
In praise of ladies dead, and lovely knights,
Then in the blazon of sweet beauty's best,
Of hand, of foot, of lip, of eye, of brow,
I see their antique pen would have expressed,
Even such a beauty as you master now.
So all of their praises are but prophecies
Of this our time, all you prefiguring,
And for they looked but with divining eyes,
They had not skill enough your worth to sing:
    For we, which now behold these present days,
    Have eyes to wonder, but lack the tongues to praise.

When in historical writings of time past and wasted away I read descriptions of beautiful women (*'wights'*), and beauty inspiring beautiful old verses praising dead ladies and chivalrous knights, then in the blaze of beauty at its most glorious of hand, foot, lip, eye and brow, I can see their antique writings would have been inspired with the beauty you possess today, so all of their praising were prophecies of this our modern time, precursor representations of all of you, and looked on with eyes to the future, but they had not the skill to express your worth. For us who exist in present days have eyes to wonder at your beauty, but lack the proper language to praise it.

Sonnet One Hundred and Sixteen

Let me not to the marriage of true minds
Admit impediments, love is not love
Which alters when it alteration finds,
Or bends with the remover to remove.
O no, it is an ever-fixed mark,
That looks on tempests and is never shaken;
It is the star to every wand'ring bark,
Whose worth's unknown, although his height be taken.
Love's not Time's fool, though rosy lips and cheeks
Within his bending sickle's compass come,
Love alters not with his brief hours and weeks,
But bears it out even to the edge of doom:
    If this be error and upon me proved,
    I never writ, nor no man ever loved.

Let me not suggest that the marriage of true minds does not have its obstacles. True love is not love until it finds itself altered when circumstances have changed, or changes direction when the lover ('*the remover*') changes to become different for the one they love and rid themselves ('*remove*') of what they once were. O no! Love is an ever fixed beacon that rides out the storms and remains unstirred. Love is a constant star that guides every ship ('*bark*'), and even though the reason why the star is there is not known, its angle in the night sky can be measured. Love is not Time's fool, even though mortal beauty finally succumbs to its destructive sweeping motion. Love does not change with the shortest of hours, or weeks, but truthfully continues on until Judgment Day. If I am wrong, and should be proved so, then I have never written about love, nor has any man ever loved.

Sonnet One Hundred and Thirty

My mistress' eyes are nothing like the sun,
Coral is far more red, than her lips red,
If snow be white, why then her breasts are dun:
If hairs be wires, black wires grow on her head:
I have seen roses damasked, red and white,
But no such roses see I in her cheeks,
And in some perfumes is there more delight,
Than in the breath that from my mistress reeks.
I love to hear her speak, yet well I know,
That music hath a far more pleasing sound:
I grant I never saw a goddess go,
My mistress when she walks treads on the ground.
    And yet by heaven, I think my love as rare,
    As any she belied with false compare.

My mistress's eyes do not shine like the sun; and coral is far redder red than her lips. If snow be white then her breasts are a disappointment (possible reference to dark brown skin colour), and if hair be of a wiry texture then my mistress's hair is black. I have seen pink roses (damask roses) but I have not seen the colour in her cheeks, and there is more a delightful scent from some perfumes than the smell of her breath. I love to hear her speak, but I know full well that music has a more pleasant sound. I admit I never saw a goddess go by, and when my mistress walks she treads the ground. And as heaven will witness, I think my love is rare as any woman accused with false comparisons.

Sonnet One Hundred and Fifty One

Love is too young to know what conscience is,
Yet who knows not conscience is born of love?
Then gentle cheater urge not my amiss,
Lest guilty of my faults thy sweet self prove.
For thou betraying me, I do betray
My nobler part to my gross body's treason,
My soul doth tell my body that he may,
Triumph in love, flesh stays no farther reason,
But rising at thy name doth point out thee,
As his triumphant prize, proud of this pride,
He is contented thy poor drudge to be,
To stand in thy affairs, fall by thy side.
    No want of conscience hold it that I call,
    Her love, for whose dear love I rise and fall.

Love (possible reference to Cupid or young love in general) is too young to understand the difference between right and wrong, but who does not know that conscience comes with the experience of love? Then lovable rogue/charmer ('*gentle cheater*') do not encourage me to admit my failings because you may find yourself guilty of the same faults that I am guilty of committing: for betraying me (possible reference to two timing) I betray the better part of me (possible reference to the soul) to the temptations of my body's desires, even though my soul tells me I can triumph in love, my flesh waits for no further justification and rises (possible reference to sexual excitement) at the mere mention of your name as my reward. Swollen with pride 'He' is happy to be your poor servant and to serve your demands when you require, and fall by your side (fall into bed beside you). It is not with any lack of conscience I consider that I can call you my love, and whose love makes me go up and down (possible double meaning of emotionally hot and cold, or sexually excited or not).

Bruno
Patron 09

Sonnet One Hundred and Fifty Four

The little Love-god lying once asleep,
Laid by his side his heart-inflaming brand,
Whilst many nymphs that vowed chaste life to keep,
Came tripping by, but in her maiden hand,
The fairest votary took up that fire,
Which many legions of true hearts had warm'd,
And so the General of hot desire,
Was sleeping by a virgin hand disarmed.
This brand she quenched in a cool well by,
Which from Love's fire took heat perpetual,
Growing a bath and healthful remedy,
For men diseased; but I my mistress' thrall,
    Came there for cure and this by that I prove,
    Love's fire heats water, water cools not love.

The little Love god (Cupid) having just laid asleep set down his heart flaming torch, whilst many nymphs who had vowed chastity came skipping by, and the hand of the fairest maiden who had avowed ('*votary*') to chastity picked up the torch (love's enflamed passion) where many other chaste maidens ('*true hearts*')had also warmed themselves; and as the General of Passions slept she laid down beside him and took his torch and quenched its fire in a nearby well to cool down, but because Love's unquenchable fire remained ablaze, this grew into a bath (or a sauna) and became a healthy cure for men diseased with fiery passions, but being my mistress's slave I came to the same place for a cure so that in doing so, I would prove that Love's passions can heat water, but water cannot cool love.

Bruno Patron is a professional artist and cartoonist whose family roots come from Northern Ireland and England. He studied Fine Art and Cartooning in Cheltenham School of Art. He has lived most of his life in London, but now lives in Northern Ireland with his daughter. This is his first illustrative publication of William Shakespeare.